FSOT Study Guide

Test Prep Secrets for the Foreign Service Officer Test (FSOT) Written Exam

Table of Contents

Introduction

There are few other professions offering the excitement or life experiences that one finds as diplomat. The job requires some serious responsibilities however, so it is to be expected that the selection process is not an easy one, and the FSOT written exam is no exception. Candidates are required to have an extensive knowledge on a wide variety of subjects such as US & world history, mathematics, economics, and public diplomacy just to name a few. We will work through all sections of the FSOT written exam, but first, let's review some basic information you need to know.

Sections on the FSOT Written Exam:
- Job Knowledge
  - This is typically regarded as the most challenging section. This is the section is almost like playing Trivial Pursuit in that a candidate simply must have a fund of knowledge and information to pull from. It is regarded by many as one of the most challenging exams to study for since there is so many possible questions to prepare for. We will help make sure you are ready though, no matter what your current skill level!

- English Expression
  - If you have taken the ACT exam before, then you are already familiar with this section. It will test your reading comprehension ability as well as your knowledge of grammar, spelling, and usage.

- Essay
  - Again, if you have taken the ACT (or SAT) then you should be familiar with the requirements for the essay section. Although the topics might be different, a quality essay depends on the same basic requirements: a clear, concise, and specific response to a prompt, free of grammar, usage, or spelling errors.

Additional Information
Keep in mind that the FSOT written exam is just one step in the process of becoming a diplomat! It is a big step and is of course indicative of whether or not a candidate will succeed in completing the entire process, but you must be aware of the other steps.

- It is imperative that you visit careers.state.gov/work and familiarize yourself with ALL of the information you can. This is the single most important and up-to-date source of information available to you, not to mention where you have to go to apply and register to take the exam. Again, we cannot stress the importance of spending as much time as necessary getting all the information you can from this website.

- Steps After Passing the FSOT Written Exam
  - Personal Narrative
    - After passing the FSOT written exam, you must submit a personal narrative. This is your chance to demonstrate why you should be considered, highlighting your strengths and abilities.

- Oral Assessment
    - After successfully submitting your Personal Narrative, you will be given an invitation for an interview which can be an entire day long process. You will have group interviews, individual interviews, writing exercises, and other group and personal exercises. Public speaking is crucial, so be sure to work on that aspect well in advance. Communication is one of the most important skills to be successful as a diplomat and is therefore weighed heavily.

- Medical Clearance, Security Clearance, Final review
    - Once you have been selected by the powers that be to continue in the application process, you will have to pass security and medical clearance. Once that is complete, your entire file is reviewed one final time to ensure that selected candidates meet all requirements. There is nothing for you to do at this point that you can prepare for, but it is worth mentioning so you are aware.

How This Book Works
We will cover all sections of the written exam and provide practice questions at the end of each chapter. Remember, this study guides is not necessarily designed to "teach" or "re-teach" you concepts, instead we will show you what is on the test, how it is formatted, and how to apply your knowledge. There is no way we could replace the amount of information you need to know and review into a single book. Carefully review all the information in each chapter before proceeding to the practice questions. Especially for the Job Knowledge section, be prepared to do outside studying. We will cover that more in detail, but it is important to be aware that a lot of reading will be necessary.

Chapter 1: Job Knowledge

The Job Knowledge tests diplomatic hopefuls on quite literally just about anything and everything, making it not just a challenging exam, but also one of the hardest tests to prepare for.

Below is a list of topic areas covered in the exam, as stated by the US State Department website careers.state.gov:

- **United States Government**: Tests general understanding of the composition and functioning of the Federal government, the Constitution and its history, the structure of Congress and its role in foreign affairs, as well as the United States political system and its role in governmental structure, formulation of government policies, and foreign affairs

- **United States Society and Culture:** Tests general understanding of major events, institutions, and governments in national history, including political and economic history, as well as national customs and culture, social issues and trends, and the influence of U.S. society on foreign policy and foreign affairs

- **World History and Geography:** Tests general understanding of significant world historical events, issues, and developments, including their impact on U.S. foreign policy, as well as knowledge of world geography and its relationship to U.S. foreign policy.

- **Economics:** Tests general understanding of basic economic principles, as well as a general understanding of economic issues and the economic system of the United States

- **Management:** Tests general understanding of basic management and supervisory techniques and methods. Includes knowledge of human psychology, leadership, motivational strategies and equal employment practices.

- **Mathematics and Statistics:** Tests basic mathematical and statistical procedures and calculations.

- **Communication**: Tests general understanding of principles of effective communication and public speaking techniques, as well as general knowledge of the common sources of information, public media and media relations.

- **Computers:** Tests general understanding of basic computer operations such as word processing, databases, spreadsheets, and preparing and using e-mail.

- **U.S. and International Political and Economic Principles, Issues and History**

- **Legislation and Laws Related to Foreign Service Issues**

- **Administrative Methods and Procedures**

- **Information and Media Resources**

As you can see, that really is an extremely wide spectrum of information to apply on a single test, let alone a single section. There is unfortunately no magic bullet for this section and just about any question is fair game....so how do you study for it? There is no way around it, you have to read, read, read, and then read some more. Some examples include:

- Go back and find notes and textbooks from US and World History and browse through them, testing yourself on practice questions you find there. You can also look online, there are hundreds of educational websites loaded with applicable information. For most people, this is the most important study method. It seems simple enough, but it is time-consuming. There is unfortunately no other way to take in as much information as you will need.

- It is imperative to keep up with current events and refresh yourself on important events in the recent years as well as history text. This information is sure to pop up on the exam. Watch or listen to the news, read the NY Times, etc.

- The Math content is actually the most straight forward aspect of this section. Simply do the practice questions in this book and you will likely be ready for the exam. If not, review high school level math and statistics until you are proficient. You won't find any curveballs or overly difficult math problems on the exam.

- If you need to, review some introductory to intermediate level lessons about computer software. Knowing the basics of Microsoft Word and Excel are helpful, but you might encounter more difficult questions as well. Some people just "get" computers and will not have to study at all, for others, this might be a more challenging aspect of the exam.

- Finally, be sure to go online and read EVERYTHING on the State Departments website. If they have information on that site, you can guarantee it is there for a reason. You can glean a lot of information that is simply hiding in plain sight.

Now, we have some practice questions to work through. If you haven't seen any example questions of what you will find on the FSOT, this will be an extremely helpful start to your studying process. You will quickly understand what a wide variety of information you will be tested on, as well as getting an idea of your current knowledge level and abilities.

Job Knowledge Practice Test Questions

1. The Vice President of the USA is also what?
    a. Secretary of Interior
    b. Speaker of the House
    c. President of the Senate
    d. Vice President of Senate

2. Which of the following names was not an influential protestant reformer?
    a. Luther
    b. Calvin
    c. Wycliffe
    d. Cramer

3. What is the 4th amendment?
    a. Right to bear arms
    b. Right to Free speech
    c. Right against unreasonable search and seizure
    d. Right against self-incrimination

4. What is considered a standard font size for most documents?
    a. 8 point
    b. 18 point
    c. 12 point
    d. 22 point

5. Which statement best summarizes the New Deal?
    a. Set of Federal programs by FDR in response to the Great Depression
    b. A new set of laws designed to increase dollar value
    c. A disbursement of entitlement programs
    d. Foreign aid initiative administered by congress in the 1940's

6. After the Vice President, who is in line to succeed a vacated Presidential seat?
    a. A pre-appointed individual from the President's cabinet
    b. Secretary of State
    c. Speaker of the House
    d. President pro tempore of the Senate

7. Adjusted minimum wage dating back to the 1960's is equitable to approximately what current day dollar value?
   a. $5
   b. $10
   c. $14
   d. $2

8. Voters directly elect which of the following?
   a. President
   b. Vice President
   c. Members of the Senate
   d. Secretary of Defense

9. What are Miranda Rights?
   a. Guarantee to educational equality
   b. A bill initiated by Senator Miranda for voting rights
   c. A law requiring police to inform the accused of their right to remain silent
   d. A law protecting rights to a fair trial

10. Although the Civil War is commonly thought to be a fight over slavery, many politicians in the South supported what?
    a. Lower taxes
    b. State's rights
    c. Agricultural subsidies
    d. Fewer restrictions on export of goods

11. What keystroke will result in copying highlighted text?
    a. Ctrl + A
    b. Ctrl + C
    c. Shift + Alt + C
    d. Alt + V

12. The ratio of output to input gives a measure of what?
    a. Proficiency
    b. effectiveness
    c. productivity
    d. operations management

13. What is the correct term for a single Excel document?
    a. Page
    b. Tab
    c. Spreadsheet

    d. Text file

14. What is the difference between a CC and BCC in emails?
    a. No difference
    b. CC can see who is on BCC list
    c. BCC can see who is on CC list
    d. BCC recipients see only their email address

15. What is the service Google, Bing, and Yahoo are most well-known for?
    a. Email
    b. Data storage
    c. Search engine
    d. Forums

16. Which file type is generally a secure option for sending in emails?
    a. .txt
    b. .docx
    c. .pdf
    d. .xml

17. To whom was Ronald Reagan addressing when he said "Tear down this wall"?
    a. Mikhail Gorbechev
    b. Vladmir Putin
    c. Joseph Stalin
    d. Dmitry Medvedev

18. A jpeg is what type of file?
    a. Text
    b. Spreadsheet
    c. Image
    d. Portable document file

19. What does "CAT" stand for such as CAT-5 or CAT-6 cable?
    a. Category
    b. Continuous Analog
    c. Constant Access
    d. None of the above

20. In Microsoft documents, what is the difference between "Save" and "Save As"?
    a. Save As creates a new document
    b. No difference
    c. Save is less secure
    d. You cannot change the document later if using Save As

21. Which of the following is not a top-level domain?
   a. .info
   b. .de
   c. .biz
   d. .tvee

22. RAM stands for what?
   a. Remote Accessible Mobile
   b. Random Access Memory
   c. Random Active Monitoring
   d. Removal All Memory

23. Where is the Hauge?
   a. Netherlands
   b. Germany
   c. Ukraine
   d. Sweden

24. USSR stands for what in terms of government?
   a. Union of Soviet Socialist Republics
   b. Uninterrupted Sustained Silent Reading
   c. Underground Security Systems Research
   d. Universal Solid State Relay

25. The Australian government has what type of government?
   a. Democracy
   b. Republic
   c. Constitutional Monarchy
   d. Parliamentary

26. Which year of Olympic games did the USA not compete?
   a. 1988
   b. 1980
   c. 1964
   d. 1968

27. What does OPEC stand for in terms of the global market?
   a. Official Private Equity Capitalization
   b. Organized Prevention and Education Conference
   c. Oceanic Processes and Export Coordination
   d. Organization of the Petroleum Exporting Countries

28. What of the following was not a peace treaty ending World War II?
    a. Paris Peace Treaty
    b. Treaty of Versailles
    c. Treaty on the Final Settlement With Respect to Germany
    d. Treaty of Peace

29. If a discount of 25% off the retail price of a desk saves Mark $45, what was desk's original price?
    a. $135.
    b. $160.
    c. $180.
    d. $210.
    e. $215.

30. What military fight is responsible for the single largest number of casualties of American lives?
    a. Iwo Jima
    b. Invasion of Normandy
    c. Battle of Gettysburg
    d. Korean War

31. What is the name of the currency used in India?
    a. Euro
    b. Rupee
    c. Real
    d. Dinar

32. Which of the following ships was not sunk at Pearl Harbor during the Japanese attack in 1941?
    a. USS Arizona
    b. USS Utah
    c. USS Oklahoma
    d. USS Maine

33. Which president signed into law the voting rights act?
    a. Kennedy
    b. LBJ
    c. Nixon
    d. Ford

34. In what year did the Korean War start?
    a. 1950
    b. 1955
    c. 1960
    d. 1953

35. What language is predominately spoken in Suadi Arabia?
    a. Persian
    b. Arabic
    c. Urdu
    d. Berber

36. During a 5-day festival, the number of visitors tripled each day. If the festival opened on a Thursday with 345 visitors, what was the attendance on that Sunday?
    a. 345.
    b. 1,035.
    c. 1,725.
    d. 9,315.

37. Which of the following is an organized teacher's union group?
    a. NRA
    b. EATA
    c. NEA
    d. LULAC

38. In what years was prohibition started?
    a. 1918
    b. 1920
    c. 1930
    d. 1933

39. The military base Camp Pendleton is located where?
    a. California
    b. Florida
    c. Virginia
    d. South Carolina

40. The US Marines is a branch of what military department?
    a. Army
    b. Navy
    c. Air Force
    d. None of the above

41. Which president signed the Defense of Marriage Act (DOMA)?
    a. Clinton
    b. HW Bush
    c. Reagan
    d. Carter

42. What generation was born from the Greatest Generation?
    a. Generation X
    b. Baby Boomers
    c. Generation Y
    d. Millennial

43. Which of the following was an influential civil rights activist assassinated at his own home?
    a. Martin Luther King Jr.
    b. Medger Evers
    c. James Chaney
    d. Viola Liuzzo

44. Who said "Ich bin ein Berliner"?
    a. Carter
    b. JFK
    c. FDR
    d. Nixon

45. What is the median of the following list of numbers: 4, 5, 7, 9, 10, and 12?
    a. 6.
    b. 7.5.
    c. 7.8.
    d. 8.
    e. 9.

46. Which of the following describes opportunity cost?
    a. The value of the next best alternative that was forgone
    b. Cost directly attributed to the production of goods
    c. Cost for the possibility of future return on investment
    d. Indirect cost such as payroll, insurance, etc

47. An amortization schedule is used commonly for what?
    a. Savings
    b. Bonds
    c. Stock Market
    d. Mortgages

48. Which of the following about FMLA is false?
    a. An employee is entitled to take FMLA after six months or more of employment.
    b. An employer must follow FMLA only if it has 50 or more employees.
    c. Under FMLA, an employee may take up to 12 weeks of job-protected, unpaid leave.
    d. In-laws are not included as "family members" under FMLA.

49. Which president was in office during the Iran-Contra scandal?
   a. Nixon
   b. Reagan
   c. Ford
   d. Carter

50. Karl Heinrich Marx is known famously for authoring what book?
   a. Mein Kampf
   b. The State and Revolution
   c. Communist Manifesto
   d. The Socialist System

51. Which describes inflation?
   a. A result of decreased demand
   b. An increase in the cost of goods
   c. A decline in the purchasing power of money
   d. Both B & C

52. Under normal conditions, when the price of a product decreases, the quantity demand will do what?
   a. increase
   b. decrease
   c. no change
   d. none of the above

53. What is something the federal reserve might do to decrease money supply?
   a. sell public bonds
   b. Buy public bonds
   c. Stop producing larger denomination bills
   d. none of the above

54. What file is Word 2007 or later?
   a. .doc
   b. .docx
   c. .ftp
   d. .txt

55. In what year did Israel take over west Jerusalem?
   a. 1200 BC
   b. 1948 AD
   c. 508 AD
   d. 1592 AD

56. A company might be in violation of the provisions of Title IV of the Civil Rights Act if their hiring practices include:
    a. Requiring educational achievements that are related to business needs
    b. Administering aptitude testing for all candidates
    c. Sorting resumes or applications by gender or race
    d. Limiting application for some positions to degreed candidates only

57. A primary use of flow charts in business documents or presentations is to
    a. Compare and contrast data
    b. Identify trends
    c. Explain relationships
    d. Summarize numerical data

58. John doesn't like Susan's political views, so he gives him a four percent pay increase instead of a six percent increase. This is an example of unethical behavior in relation to _____ management.
    a. Business-information
    b. Human-resources
    c. Capital-assets
    d. Financial-services

59. According to equity theory, after an employee receives a reward for performance, what is the next step the employee takes in the motivation process?
    a. Renegotiating new valued rewards for the next performance period
    b. Comparing the reward with a self-selected comparison group or person
    c. Reducing productivity briefly while enjoying the earned reward
    d. Expecting an increase in future rewards

60. What is sunk cost?
    a. A cost for which there will never be a return on investment
    b. A cost that has already been incurred, so cannot be directly recovered
    c. A term for nitial start-up investment
    d. Cost for which there will be less than 80% ROI

61. The process used to settle labor disputes with the assistance of a neutral third party, who is authorized to determine a solution, is known as
    a. arbitration
    b. conciliation
    c. mediation
    d. collective bargaining

62. If Lynn can type a page in p minutes, how many pages can she do in 5 minutes?
   a) $5/p$.
   b) $p - 5$.
   c) $p + 5$.
   d) $p/5$.

63. Round 907.457 to the nearest tens place.
   a. 908.0.
   b. 910.
   c. 907.5.
   d. 900.
   e. 907.46.

64. Find $0.12 \div 1$.
   a. 12.
   b. 1.2.
   c. .12.
   d. .012.
   e. .0012.

65. There are 12 more apples than oranges in a basket of 36 apples and oranges. How many apples are in the basket?
   a. 12.
   b. 15.
   c. 24.
   d. 28.
   e. 36.

66. In what year was space shuttle Discovery decommissioned?
   a. 1998
   b. 2012
   c. 2006
   d. 2010

67. How long will Lucy have to wait before for her $2,500 invested at 6% earns $600 in simple interest?
   a. 2 years.
   b. 3 years.
   c. 4 years.
   d. 5 years.

68. Grace has 16 jellybeans in her pocket. She has 8 red ones, 4 green ones, and 4 blue ones. What is the minimum number of jellybeans she must take out of her pocket to ensure that she has one of each color?
    a. 4.
    b. 8.
    c. 12.
    d. 13.

69. John is traveling to a meeting that is 28 miles away. He needs to be there in 30 minutes. How fast does he need to go in order to make it to the meeting on time?
    a. 25 mph.
    b. 37 mph.
    c. 41 mph.
    d. 56 mph

70. In an Excel document, what equation will add the contents of highlighted cells?
    a. =SUM(xx)
    b. =ADD
    c. SUM = (xx + xx)
    d. CTRL + A

1. C
2. D
3. C
4. C
5. A
6. C
7. A
8. C
9. C
10. B
11. B
12. C
13. C
14. D
15. C
16. C
17. A
18. C
19. A
20. A
21. D
22. B
23. A
24. A
25. C
26. B
27. D
28. B
29. C
30. C
31. B
32. D
33. B
34. A
35. B
36. D
37. C
38. B
39. A

40. B
41. A
42. B
43. B
44. B
45. D
46. A
47. D
48. A
49. B
50. C
51. D
52. A
53. B
54. B
55. B
56. C
57. C
58. B
59. B
60. B
61. A
62. A
63. B
64. C
65. C
66. B
67. C
68. D
69. D
70. A

Chapter 2: English Expression

In the English Expression portion of the exam, you will need to demonstrate your competency in both the usage and mechanics of the English language, as well as rhetorical skills.

The **usage/mechanics questions** cover the following concepts:

- **Punctuation:** Apostrophes, colons, semi-colons, commas, dashes, hyphens, quotation marks, parentheses, and their functions in clarifying the meaning of text selections.

- **Basic Grammar:** Verbs, adverbs, adjectives, subject-verb agreement, pronoun-antecedent agreement, and the proper use of connectives.

- **Sentence Structure:** Clauses, modifiers, parallelism, consistency in tense, and point-of-view.

Remember the Reading Placement section? The **rhetorical questions** are quite similar. You will be given a passage to read, with questions covering either the entire passage, or separate parts. You will demonstrate your knowledge of:

- **Strategy:** The author's choice of supporting material – if is it effective, applicable, and ample in quality and quantity.

- **Style:** The best choice of adjectives, word order, or alternative wording that most concisely articulates an idea.

- **Organization:** Sentence arrangement within a paragraph, paragraph arrangement within the passage, the need for further information, and the presence of unnecessary information.

Tips

As with all the section tests, you have to know your English grammar. This exam will not be unjustly 'sneaky,' but you do have to be observant and thorough enough to catch errors. Here are some tips to help improve your score.

The Three Main No-No's.
There are three main things the test is stringent about:

1. **Redundancy** (repetitious text or words).

2. **Irrelevance** (words or ideas not directly or logically associated with the purpose or main idea).

3. **Wordiness** (drawing out a sentence).

Peruse the entire passage paragraph before answering any of the questions.
Many study guides will tell you not to read the entire passage before answering the usage/mechanics questions; however, that approach lends to a greater possibility of error. The overall meaning or purpose

23

of the paragraph can change the propriety of the highlighted text. For example, looking at just the sentence containing the highlighted word group may cause you to misinterpret the intended parallels or point of view.

Read every word of every question.
Don't assume that you know what is being asked after reading the first few words. Remember, one word at the end of a sentence can change the entire meaning.

Read all the answer choices before making a selection.
Some choices will be partially correct (pertaining to a part, but not all, of the passage) and are intended to catch the eye of the sloppy tester. Note the differences between your answer choices; sometimes they are very subtle.

Understand transitions.
The exam will require you to recognize the shortest, most proper way to go from one sentence or paragraph to another.

Familiarize yourself with various styles of writing.
The passages may be excerpts from anything: poetry, cause/effect essays, comparison /contrast essays, definition essays, description essays, narration essays, persuasive essays, or process analysis essays.

Learn the directions.
Knowing the directions before test day saves valuable minutes. It enables you to glance quickly at the directions and start answering questions.

And, most importantly, review! Most people cannot learn sentence rules by memorization, like they do math or science. Instead, the best way to learn how sentences fit together is by reading! Studying the following terms and rules will help a great deal.

Syntax

"Syntax" refers to the rules for the formation of grammatical sentences in a language. (That definition, while correct, is pretty stuffy. Basically, "syntax" means "sentence structure.")

It's very easy to understand why syntax is important. In order to convey meaningful information in a way that makes sense, sentences need to comply with the rules of grammar. Most readers and speakers have a general understanding of these rules; it's crucial for you to demonstrate syntactical competency as well.

Let's look at an example.

> "When Heidi woke up in the morning, she noticed three things which disturbed her greatly: the first being that she was a ghost."

But what if we started the sentence this way?

> "The first being that she was a ghost: she noticed three things when Heidi woke up which disturbed her greatly."

After reading this sentence, you would probably be utterly confused and, most likely, unwilling to continue reading. Why would you have this reaction? Because the sentence doesn't make grammatical sense.

Now the above example is very easy. But chances are that the questions on the exam may be a bit harder. Therefore, it's important that you understand the top five grammatical rules:

1. Sentences that maintain the subject-verb-object order are more readable than those which do not.

2. When you can, place the subject and the verb close together in a sentence.

3. Keep modifiers and the words that they modify close together in a sentence.

4. Try to put people in the subject position in a sentence.

5. Put old information first in a sentence and new information last.

Nouns, Pronouns, Verbs, Adjectives, and Adverbs

Nouns
Nouns are people, places, or things. They are typically the subject of a sentence. For example, "The hospital was very clean." The noun is "hospital;" it is the "place."

Pronouns
Pronouns essentially "replace" nouns. This allows a sentence to not sound repetitive. Take the sentence: "Sam stayed home from school because Sam was not feeling well." The word "Sam" appears twice in the same sentence. Instead, you can use a pronoun and say, "Sam stayed at home because *he* did not feel well." Sounds much better, right?

Most Common Pronouns:

- I, me, mine, my.

- You, your, yours.

- He, him, his.

- She, her, hers.

- It, its.

- We, us, our, ours.

- They, them, their, theirs.

25

Verbs

Remember the old commercial, "Verb: It's what you do"? That sums up verbs in a nutshell! Verbs are the "action" of a sentence; verbs "do" things.

They can, however, be quite tricky. Depending on the subject of a sentence, the tense of the word (past, present, future, etc.), and whether or not they are regular or irregular, verbs have many variations.

Example: "He runs to second base." The verb is "runs." This is a "regular verb."

Example: "I am 7 years old." The verb in this case is "am." This is an "irregular verb."

As mentioned, verbs must use the correct tense – and that tense must remain the same throughout the sentence. "I was baking cookies and eat some dough." That sounded strange, didn't it? That's because the two verbs "baking" and "eat" are presented in different tenses. "Was baking" occurred in the past; "eat," on the other hand, occurs in the present. Instead, it should be "**ate** some dough."

Adjectives

Adjectives are words that describe a noun and give more information. Take the sentence: "The boy hit the ball." If you want to know more about the noun "boy," then you could use an adjective to describe it. "The **little** boy hit the ball." An adjective simply provides more information about a noun or subject in a sentence.

Adverbs

For some reason, many people have a difficult time with adverbs – but don't worry! They are really quite simple. Adverbs are similar to adjectives in that they provide more information; however, they describe verbs, adjectives, and even other adverbs. They do **not** describe nouns – that's an adjective's job.

Take the sentence: "The doctor said she hired a new employee."

It would give more information to say: "The doctor said she **recently** hired a new employee." Now we know more about *how* the action was executed. Adverbs typically describe when or how something has happened, how it looks, how it feels, etc.

Good vs. Well

A very common mistake that people make concerning adverbs is the misuse of the word "good."

"Good" is an adjective – things taste good, look good, and smell good. "Good" can even be a noun – "Superman does good" – when the word is speaking about "good" vs. "evil." HOWEVER, "good" is never an adverb.

People commonly say things like, "I did really good on that test," or, "I'm good." Ugh! This is NOT the correct way to speak! In those sentences, the word "good" is being used to describe an action: how a person **did**, or how a person **is**. Therefore, the adverb "well" should be used. "I did really **well** on that test." "I'm **well**."

The correct use of "well" and "good" can make or break a person's impression of your grammar – make sure to always speak correctly!

Study Tips for Improving Vocabulary and Grammar

1. You're probably pretty computer savvy and know the Internet very well. Visit the Online Writing Lab website, which is sponsored by Purdue University, at http://owl.english.purdue.edu. This site provides you with an excellent overview of syntax, writing style, and strategy. It also has helpful and lengthy review sections that include multiple-choice "Test Your Knowledge" quizzes, which provide immediate answers to the questions.

2. It's beneficial to read the entire passage first to determine its intended meaning BEFORE you attempt to answer any questions. Doing so provides you with key insight into a passage's syntax (especially verb tense, subject-verb agreement, modifier placement, writing style, and punctuation).

3. When you answer a question, use the "Process-of-Elimination Method" to determine the best answer. Try each of the four answers and determine which one BEST fits with the meaning of the paragraph. Find the BEST answer. Chances are that the BEST answer is the CORRECT answer.

Test Your Knowledge: English Expression

Directions:
In the passages that follow, certain words and phrases are underlined and numbered. In the right-hand column, you will find alternatives for each underlined part. You are to choose the one that best expresses the idea, makes the statement appropriate for standard written English, or is worded most consistently with the style and tone of the passage as a whole. If you think the original version is best, choose option A., which is the same as the original version. You may also find questions about a section of the passage, or about the passage as a whole. These questions do not refer to an underlined portion of the passage, but rather are identified by a number or numbers. For each question, choose the alternative you consider best and circle the letter of that choice. Read each passage through once before you begin to answer the questions that accompany it. You cannot determine most answers without reading several sentences beyond the question. Be sure that you have read far enough ahead each time you choose an alternative.

PASSAGE I: Examining my Ecological Footprint

Examining the impact my lifestyle has on the earth's resources is <u>a fascinating and valuable thing to do</u>. According to the Earth
1

Day Network ecological footprint calculator created by the Sierra Club, it would take four planet earths to sustain the human population if everyone used as many resources as I do. My "ecological footprint," or the amount of productive area of the earth that is required to produce the resources I consume, <u>must then be much</u> larger
2

<u>like those of</u> most of the population.
3
It is hard to balance the luxuries and opportunities I

1.

a) NO CHANGE
b) a fascinating or valuable thing to do.
c) fascinating to do and also valuable to do.
d) done to be fascinating or valuable.

2.

f) NO CHANGE
g) would have been
h) much
j) was much

3.

a) NO CHANGE
b) than those of
c) than footprints of
d) as the footprints of

28

have available to <u>me: with</u> doing what I know to be
4
better from an ecological standpoint.

One's ecological footprint is <u>measured with</u>
5
accounting for different factors such as how often

and how far one drives and travels by air, what kind

of structure one lives in, and what kind of goods one

consumes (and how far those consumer goods travel

across the globe). For example, a person who lives

in a freestanding home, which uses more energy to

heat and cool than an apartment in a building does;

who travels internationally several times per year;

and who eats exotic, out-of-season foods which

must be shipped in from other countries, rather than

locally grown and raised food <u>which is</u> in season,
6
would have a large ecological footprint.

| 7 |

4.

   f) NO CHANGE
   g) me, with
   h) me; with
   j) me with

5.

   a) NO CHANGE
   b) measured by
   c) measured with
   d) measured of

6.

   f) NO CHANGE
   g) that are
   h) those are
   j) which are

7. The last sentence in the above
paragraph could be improved by:

   a) Being broken into short
      sentences.
   b) Being moved to the beginning
      of the paragraph.
   c) Including information about
      how the footprint is calculated.
   d) Taking out "for example" at
      the beginning of the sentence.

Although I get points for recycling, <u>my</u>

<u>use of</u> public transportation, and living in an
8

apartment complex rather than a free-standing

residence; my footprint expands when it is taken

into account my not-entirely-local diet, my

occasional use of a car, my three magazine

subscriptions, and my history of flying more than

ten hours a year. These are all examples of things

that use a large amount of resources.

| 9 |

This examination of the impact my lifestyle <u>has</u>

<u>on the earth's resources</u> is fascinating and valuable
10

to me. It is fairly easy for me to recycle, so I do it,

8.
f) NO CHANGE
g) use of
h) using
j) my using

9. The writer wants to add a sentence to the end of the paragraph that encourages others to calculate their own ecological footprint. Which of the following sentences would best accomplish this?

a) There are many different ways that we use resources that may be surprising.
b) Other things I do that use high amounts of resources include using a dryer for my laundry and leaving appliances plugged in when I'm out of the house.
c) Sources of waste are often surprising; you can calculate your own ecological footprint online at myfootprint.org.
d) Sometimes the best way to reduce one's use of resources is to travel less.

10.
f) NO CHANGE
g) on the resources of the planet
h) had on the earth's resources
j) has on the earth resources

but it would be much harder to <u>forgoing</u> the
                                  11

opportunity to travel by plane or eat my favorite

<u>fruits; that</u> have been flown to the supermarket from
     12

a different country. I feel that realizing just how

unfair my share of the <u>earths' resources has</u> been
                   13

should help me to change at least some of my bad

habit. Perhaps if we were all made aware of the true

cost of our habits, actions, and <u>choices, people</u>
                      14

would be more likely to take steps to reduce <u>his or</u>
                      15

<u>her</u> consumption of the earth's resources.

11.
    a) NO CHANGE
    b) forgo
    c) have forgone
    d) not forgo

12.
    f) NO CHANGE
    g) fruits, that
    h) fruits that
    j) fruits: that

13.
    a) NO CHANGE
    b) earth's resources has
    c) earths' resources have
    d) earth's resources have

14.
    f) NO CHANGE
    g) choices. People
    h) choices; people
    j) than people

15.
    a) NO CHANGE
    b) our
    c) their
    d) one's

PASSAGE II
The Sculptor Augusta Savage

Augusta <u>Savage were</u> a world-famous African-
16

American sculptor. <u>Born in Florida,</u> her first formal
17
art training was in New York City at Cooper Union,

the school recommended to her by Solon Gorglum.

<u>While she studied,</u> she supported herself by doing
18
odd jobs, including clerking and working in

laundries. In 1926 she exhibited her work at the

Sesquicentennial Exposition in Philadelphia. That

same year she was awarded a scholarship to study in

Rome. However, she was unable to accept the

award because she could not raise the money <u>she

would have needed</u> to live there.
19

When she returned to the United States, she

exhibited her work at several important galleries. <u>In

addition to her own work,</u> Augusta Savage taught
20
art classes in Harlem. During the Depression, she

helped African- American artists to enroll in the

Works Progress Administration arts project.

16.

f) NO CHANGE
g) Savage, was
h) Savage, were
j) Savage was

17.

a) NO CHANGE
b) She was born in Florida,
c) While being born inFlorida,
d) Although she was born in Florida,

18.

f) NO CHANGE
g) While she studied
h) After studying
j) She studied while

19.

a) NO CHANGE
b) she would need
c) she needed
d) she needs

20.

f) NO CHANGE
g) Additional to creating her own work,
h) Additionally to her own work,
j) In addition to creating her own work,

Throughout her career, she was an active

spokesperson for African-American artists in the

United States. She also was one of the principal
                21
organizers of the Harlem Artists Guild.

In 1923 Savage, applied for a summer art
     22
program sponsored by the French government;

despite being more than qualified, she was turned

down by the international judging committee, solely

because of her race. Savage was deeply upset,

questioning the committee, beginning the first of
23

many public fights for equal rights in her life. The

incident got press coverage on both sides of the

Atlantic, and eventually the sole supportive

committee member, sculptor Hermon Atkins

MacNeil—who at one time had shared a studio with

Henry Ossawa Tanner—invited her to study with
                                24
him.

21. The author wants to combine the last two sentences of this paragraph. What is the best way to rewrite the underlined portion?

   a) States; she also
   b) States, although she also
   c) States, and also
   d) States and she

22.
   f) NO CHANGE
   g) 1923 Savage
   h) 1923, Savage
   j) 1923; Savage

23.
   a) NO CHANGE
   b) and questioned
   c) and questioning
   d) and so she questioned

24.
   f) NO CHANGE
   g) invited her to study with himself
   h) invited him to study with her
   j) gave her an invitation to study with him

25.

33

She later cite him as one of her teachers.
25

In 1939, Augusta Savage received a commission from the World's Fair and created a 16 foot tall plaster sculpture called *Lift Ev'ry Voice and Sing.* Savage did not have any funds for a bronze cast, or even to move and store it, and it was
26
destroyed by bulldozers at the close of the fair. However, small metal and plaster souvenir copies of the sculpture has survived.
27

| 28 |

Perhaps Savage's more indelible legacy is the work of the students whom she taught in her studio, the Savage Studio of Arts and Crafts. Her students included Jacob Lawrence, Norman Lewis, and Gwendolyn Knight. Lawrence was a Cubist painter whose work is hosted in museums across the country. Lewis was an Abstract Expressionist painter who often dealt with music and jazz in

a) NO CHANGE
b) was citing
c) citing
d) cited

26.
f) NO CHANGE
g) the plaster
h) them
j) her

27.
a) NO CHANGE
b) have
c) were
d) would

28. Which sentence would best fit at the beginning of the paragraph that now begins "In 1939"?

f) Her education in the arts was substantial after working with so many high profit sculptors.
g) African-Americans were still facing terrible discrimination at the end of the 1930's.
h) The World's Fair is a huge art exhibit that occurs every two to four years.
j) Throughout the 1930's, her profile as an artist continued to grow.

abstract ways. <u>Knight who was born in Barbados</u>
29
founded an organization to support young artists.

Augusta Savage <u>worked tireless</u> to teach these
30
artists, help them to secure funding, and support

their careers.

29.
   a) NO CHANGE
   b) Knight, who was born in Barbados
   c) Knight who was born in Barbados,
   d) Knight, who was born in Barbados,

30.
   f)   NO CHANGE
   g) worked tirelessly
   h) worked herself tireless
   j) was working tireless

PASSAGE III
History of Art for Beginners and Students – Ancient Painting

The following passage is adapted from Clara Erskine Clément's History of Art for Beginners and Students, first published in 1887 (public domain; errors inserted for the purposes of crafting questions).

In speaking of art we often contrast the useful or mechanical arts with the Fine Arts; by these terms we denote the difference between the arts which are used in making such things as are necessary and useful in civilized life, and the arts by which ornamental and beautiful <u>things made.</u> The fine
31

arts are Architecture, Sculpture, Painting, Poetry, and Music, and though we could live if none of these <u>existed, yet</u> life would be far from the pleasant
32

experience that it is often <u>made to be</u> through the
33
enjoyment of these arts.

Of course, forms of art can be both fine and useful. While painting belongs to the fine or beautiful arts, it is a very useful art in many ways. For example, when a school-book is illustrated, how much more easily we understand the subject we are studying through the help we get from pictures of objects or places that we have not otherwise seen.

31.
a) NO CHANGE
b) things.
c) things are made.
d) things are used.

32.
f) NO CHANGE
g) existed,
h) yet,
j) existed and yet

33.
a) NO CHANGE
b) made out to be
c) made
d) is

Pictures of natural scenery bring all countries before our eyes in such a way that by looking at <u>it</u>, while
34
reading books of travel, we may know a great deal more about lands we have never seen, and may never be able to visit.

[35]

34.
   f) NO CHANGE
   g) those
   h) them
   j) one

35. Which of the following sentences could be added to the above paragraph to give another example of how pictures are useful as well as decorative?

   a) Pictures are not useful, however, when they distract students from the purpose of a text.
   b) Pictures can be a beautiful addition to our homes.
   c) Doctors often use pictures when studying the body to help them learn organs and systems.
   d) This is helpful because people really don't travel to other lands anymore.

St. Augustine, who wrote in the fourth <u>century,</u>
36
<u>says</u> that "pictures are the books of the simple or unlearned." This is just as true now as then, and we should regard pictures as one of the best methods for teaching. The cultivation of the imagination is very <u>important because for</u> this way
37
we can add much to our individual happiness. Thus one of the uses of pictures is that they give us a clear idea of what we have not seen; a second use is

36.
   f) NO CHANGE
   g) century says
   h) century said
   j) century, said

37.
   a) NO CHANGE
   b) important, because in
   c) important, because for
   d) important; in

38.

that they are exciting to our imaginations, and often
38
help us to forget disagreeable circumstances and

unpleasant surroundings. Through this power, if we

are in a dark, narrow street, in a house which is not

to our liking, or in the midst of any unpleasant
39
happenings, we are able to fix our thoughts upon a

photograph or picture that may be there, and

we are able to imagine ourselves far, far

away, in some spot where nature makes everything

pleasant and soothes us into forgetfulness of all that

makes us unhappy. Many an invalid—many

an unfortunate person is made content by pictures

during hours that would otherwise be wretched.
40

This is the result of cultivating the imagination and

when this is done, we have a source of pleasure
41

within ourselves which can never be taken from

us.

  It often happens that we see two people doing
42
the same work and are situated in the same way in

f) NO CHANGE
g) exciting
h) excite
j) excited

39. If the writer deletes this section of this sentence, what will be lost?

  a) Nothing; the meaning of the sentence will not change.
  b) The argument that pictures are useful.
  c) The example of pictures being educational.
  d) The generalization of   the specific example to all unpleasant circumstances.

40.

  f) NO CHANGE
  g) tend to be
  h) however be
  j) be

41.
  a) NO CHANGE
  b) imagination so when
  c) imagination, and when
  d) imagination; when

42.
  f) NO CHANGE
  g) are doing
  h) who do
  j) done

the world, but who are different in their <u>manner</u>
43
<u>one</u> is light-hearted and happy, the other sullen and

sad. If you can find out the truth, it will be that

the sad one is matter-of-fact, and has no

imagination—he can only think of his work and

what concerns him personally; but the merry one

would surprise you if you could read his thoughts—

if you could know the distances <u>they have</u> passed
44

over, and what a vast difference there is between his

thought and his work. So while it is natural for

almost everyone to exclaim <u>joyful</u> at the beauty of
45
 pictures, and to enjoy looking at them simply, I

wish my readers to think of their uses also, and

understand the benefits that may be derived from

them.

43.
   a) NO CHANGE
   b) manner; one
   c) manner. One
   d) manner: one

44.
   f) NO CHANGE
   g) he has
   h) it has
   j) you have

45.
   a) NO CHANGE
   b) joyfully
   c) joy
   d) with joy

Test Your Knowledge: Writing Skills Placement – Answers

1. a)

2. f)

3. b)

4. j)

5. b)

6. f)

7. a)

8. h) This is an instance of parallelism, where you want verbs in a list in a sentence to have the same form.

9. c)

10. f)

11. b)

12. h)

13. b)

14. f)

15. c)

16. j)

17. d) This is an example of a misplaced modifier and needs to be edited.

18. f)

19. a)

20. j)

21. c)

22. h)

23. b)

24. f)

25. d)

26. g)

27. b)

28. j) This sentence best follows the topic of the passage while leading into the new information in this paragraph.

29. d)

30. g)

31. c)

32. g)

33. d)

34. h)

35. c)

36. f)

37. b)

38. h)

39. d)

40. f)

41. c)

42. h)

43. d)

44. f)

45. b)

Chapter 3: Essay

An Effective Essay Demonstrates:

1. Insightful and effective development of a point-of-view on the issue.

2. Critical thinking skills. For example: Two oppositions are given; instead of siding with one, you provide examples in which both would be appropriate.

3. Organization. It is clearly focused and displays a smooth progression of ideas.

4. Supportive information. If a statement is made, it is followed by examples, reasons, or other supporting evidence.

5. Skillful use of varied, accurate, and apt vocabulary.

6. Sentence variety. (Not every sentence follows a "subject-verb" pattern. Mix it up!)

7. Proper grammar and spelling.

Things to Keep in Mind While Writing Your Essay

- **Rhetorical Force**: This factor judges how coherently the writer composes their essay. How clear is the idea or argument that is being presented?

- **Organization**: The writing must have a logical order, so that the reader can easily follow along and understand the main points being made.

- **Support and Development**: The use and quality of supporting arguments and information. Essays should not be vague.

- **Usage**: Essays should demonstrate a competent command of word choice, showing both accuracy and quality in the words used.

- **Structure and Convention**: Essays should be free of errors, including: spelling, punctuation, capitalization, sentence structure, etc.

- **Appropriateness**: Essays should be written in a style appropriate for the topic; they should also contain material appropriate for both the topic and the audience.

- **Timing**: You will have a limited time within which to write your essay. Pace yourself; and practice, practice, practice!

In this chapter, we will provide a sample essay prompt, followed by four short sample responses. The four sample responses each display different qualities of work; an explanation will follow each sample, explaining what score it would have earned and why.

Essay Examples and Evaluations

Prompt:
Research tells us that what children learn in their earliest years is very important to their future success in school. Because of this, public schools all over the country are starting to offer Pre-Kindergarten classes.

What are the benefits of starting school early? What are some of the problems you see in sending four-year-olds to school?

Write a composition in which you weigh the pros and cons of public school education for Pre-Kindergartners. Give reasons and specific examples to support your opinion. There is no specific word limit for your composition, but it should be long enough to give a clear and complete presentation of your ideas.

Sample High-Quality Essay

Today, more and more four-year-olds are joining their big brothers and sisters on the school bus and going to Pre-Kindergarten. Although the benefits of starting school early are clear, it is also clear that Pre-K is not for every child.

The students who are successful in Pre-K are ahead when they start kindergarten. Pre-K teaches them to play well with others. Even though it does not teach skills like reading and writing, it does help to prepare students for "real" school. Pre-K students sing songs, dance, paint and draw, climb and run. They learn to share and to follow directions. They tell stories and answer questions, and as they do, they add new words to their vocabularies. Pre-K can also give students experiences they might not get at home. They might take trips to the zoo or the farm, have visits from musicians or scientists, and so on. These experiences help the students better understand the world.

There are, however, some real differences among children of this age. Some four-year-olds are just not ready for the structure of school life. Some have a hard time leaving home, even for only three or four hours a day. Other children may already be getting a great preschool education at home or in daycare.

While you weigh the advantages and disadvantages of Pre-K, it is safe to say that each child is different. For some children, it is a wonderful introduction to the world of school. But others may not or should not be forced to attend Pre-K.

Evaluation of Sample High-Quality Essay
This paper is clearly organized and has stated a definite point of view. The paper opens with an introduction and closes with a conclusion. The introduction and conclusion combine an expression of the writer's opinion. Connections to the writer's opinion are made throughout the paper.

Sample Medium/Low-Quality Essay

Just like everything in life, there are pros and cons to early childhood education. Pre-K classes work for many children, but they aren't for everyone. The plusses of Pre-K are obvious. Pre-K children learn many skills that will help them in kindergarten and later on. Probably the most important thing they learn is how to follow directions. This is a skill they will need at all stages of their life.

Other plusses include simple tasks like cutting, coloring in the lines, and learning capital letters. Many children don't get these skills at home. They need Pre-K to prepare them for kindergarten.

The minuses of Pre-K are not as obvious, but they are real. Children at this young age need the comfort of home. They need to spend time with parents, not strangers. They need that security. If parents are able to, they can give children the background they need to do well in school.

Other minuses include the fact that a lot of four year-old children can't handle school. They don't have the maturaty to sit still, pay attention, or share with others. Given another year, they may mature enough to do just fine in school. Sometimes it's better just to wait.

So there are definitely good things about Pre-K programs in our public schools, and I would definitely want to see one in our local schools. However, I think parents should decide whether their children are ready for a Pre-K education or not.

Evaluation of Sample Medium-Quality Essay

This paper has an identifiable organization plan, with pros and cons listed in order. The development is easy to understand, if not somewhat simplistic. The language of the paper is uneven, with some vague turns of phrase: "Just like everything in life," "definitely some good things." The word "maturity" is also misspelled. However, the essay is clear and controlled, and generally follows written conventions. If the writer had included more developed and explicit examples and used more varied words, this paper might have earned a higher score.

Sample Extremely Low-Quality Essay

What are benefits? What are some of problems with sending four-year-olds to school? Well, for one problem, its hard to see how little kids would do with all those big kids around at the school. They might get bullyed or lern bad habits, so I wouldnt want my four year old around those big kids on the bus and so on. Its hard to see how that could be good for a four year old. In our area we do have Pre-Kindergarten at our school but you dont have to go there a lot of kids in the program, I think about 50 or more, you see them a lot on the play ground mostly all you see them do is play around so its hard to see how that could be too usefull. They could play around at home just as easy. A reason for not doing Pre-Kindergarten is then what do you learn in Kindergarten. Why go do the same thing two years when you could just do one year when your a little bit bigger (older). I wonder do the people who want Pre- Kindergarten just want there kids out of the house or a baby sitter for there kids. Its hard to see why do we have to pay for that. I dont even know if Kindergarten is so usefull anyway, not like first grade where you actially learn something. So I would say theres lots of problems with Pre-Kindergarten.

Evaluation of Sample Low-Quality Essay

This paper barely responds to the prompt. It gives reasons not to support Pre-K instruction, but it does not present any benefits of starting school early. The writer repeats certain phrases ("It's hard to see") to no real effect, and the faulty spelling, grammar, and punctuation significantly impede understanding. Several sentences wander off the topic entirely ("there a lot of kids in the program, I think about 50 or more, you see them a lot on the playground.", "I dont even know if Kindergarten is so usefull anyway, not like first grade where you actially learn something."). Instead of opening with an introduction, the writer simply lifts phrases from the prompt. The conclusion states the writer's opinion, but the reasons behind it are illogical and vague. Rather than organizing the essay in paragraph form, the writer has written a single, run-on paragraph. The lack of organization, weak language skills, and failure to address the prompt earn this essay a low score.

Test Your Knowledge: Writing Essay

Prompt One

Provided below is an excerpt and a question. Use the excerpt to prompt your thinking, and then plan and write an essay by answering the question from your perspective. Be sure to provide evidence.

- *General George S. Patton Jr. is quoted as having said, "No good decision was ever made in a swivel chair."*

Is it necessary to be directly in a situation in order to best understand what must be done?

Prompt Two

Provided below is an excerpt and a question. Use the excerpt to prompt your thinking, and then plan and write an essay by answering the question from your perspective. Be sure to provide evidence.

- *In The Dispossessed, published in 1974, groundbreaking science fiction author Ursula K. LeGuin wrote, "You can't crush ideas by suppressing them. You can only crush them by ignoring them."*

Is it possible to get rid of an idea?

Prompt Three

Provided below is an excerpt and a question. Use the excerpt to prompt your thinking, and then plan and write an essay by answering the question from your perspective. Be sure to provide evidence.

- *"The paradox of education is precisely this -- that as one begins to become conscious one begins to examine the society in which he is being educated." James Baldwin (1924-1987), American novelist, poet, and social critic*

Does a successful education require the examination of one's own society?

Test Your Knowledge: Essay – Answers

The following pages hold sample scored essays for topics one, two, and three. Look for: reasoning, examples, word usage, coherency, and detail. There are no "right" answers on your essay; the most important factor is that the argument be well developed.

Essays for Prompt One

Is it necessary to be directly in a situation to best understand what must be done?

High Quality:

General George Patton was speaking of war when he noted that "no good decision was ever made in a swivel chair;" however, that observation applies to situations beyond battle. While a big-picture perspective is useful in analyzing situations and deciding how to act, an on-the-ground outlook is essential. In matters of politics, and technology, to name two, the best-laid plans usually have to be changed to respond to changing circumstances.

One example which illustrates the necessity of on-the-ground action is the famous space flight of Apollo 13. Before launch, all plans were worked out to get the manned mission to the moon and back. However, due to a fluke set of circumstances – an oxygen tank explosion and the resulting technical problems – the plans had to change. The successful return of Apollo 13 and the survival of its crew would not have been possible without the quick thinking of the men on board. They first noticed the incident, well before the technical crew in Houston would have detected it from Earth. While the work of the technical crew was of course key as well, without the astronauts on board the ship to implement an emergency plan, the mission would surely have been lost.

Just as there are often unforeseen circumstances when implementing technology, politics can also be unpredictable. For example, the Cuban Missile Crisis in 1962 required immediate, on-the-ground decision making by the leaders of the United States. Prior to the Cold War standoff, President Kennedy and his advisors had already decided their hardline position against Soviet weapons expansion in the Western hemisphere. The Monroe Doctrine, status quo since the 1920s, held that European countries should not practice their influence in the Americas. The Soviet Union tested this line by establishing intermediate-range missiles on the island of Cuba. President Kennedy could not simply hold to the established wisdom, because the true limits had never been tested. Instead, to stave off the threat of attack, he was forced to act immediately as events unfolded to preserve the safety of American lives. The crisis unfolded minute-by-minute, with formerly confident advisors unsure of the smartest step. Eventually, after thirteen tense days, the leaders were able to reach a peaceful conclusion.

What these events of the 1960s illustrate is that the best laid plans are often rendered useless by an unfolding situation. For crises to be resolved, whether they be in war, technology, or politics; leaders must have level heads in the moment with up-to-date information. Therefore, plans established in advance by those in swivel chairs with level heads are not always the best plans to follow. History has shown us that we must be able to think on our feet as unforeseen situations unfold.

Medium/Low Quality:

It is often necessary to be directly on the ground as a situation unfolds to know what is best do to. This is because situations can be unpredictable and what you previously thought was the best course of action, is not always so. This can be seen in the unfolding events of the 1962 Cuban Missile Crisis.

The Cuban Missile Crisis happened in 1962, during the presidency of John F. Kennedy, when Nikita Khrushchev, president of the Soviet Union, developed an intermediate-range missile base on the island of Cuba, within range of the United States. Since the Monroe Doctrine in the 1920s, the United States leaders have declared that they would not tolerate this kind of aggression. However, the decisions that had been made by leaders in the past, removed from the situation, were no longer relevant. It was necessary for President Kennedy to make decisions as events unfolded.

As the Cuban Missile Crisis shows us, at turning points in history decisions have to be made as events unfold by those who are in the middle of a situation. Otherwise, we would all be acting according to what those in the past and those removed from the challenge thought was best. Following the Monroe Doctrine could have resulted in unnecessary violence.

Essays for Prompt Two

Is it possible to get rid of an idea?

High Quality:

The suppression of ideas has been attempted over and over throughout history by different oppressive regimes. This theme has been explored as well in literature, through such dystopian works as 1984 and Fahrenheit 451. But these histories and stories always play out the same way: eventually, the repressed idea bubbles to the surface and triumphs. Ursula K. LeGuin acknowledged this by saying that ideas can be crushed not by suppression, but by omission.

In Aldous Huxley's novel <u>Brave New World</u>, the world government maintains order not by governing people strictly and policing their ideas, but by distracting them. Consumption is the highest value of the society. When an outsider to the society comes in and questions it, he is exiled – not to punish him, but to remove his influence from society. The government of the dystopia has learned that the best way to maintain control is to keep citizens unaware of other, outside ideas. This theme resonates with a modern audience more than other, more authoritarian tales of dystopia because in our society, we are less controlled than we are influenced and persuaded.

Repressing ideas through harsh authoritarian rule has proven time and again to be ultimately fruitless. For example, in Soviet Russia during the 1920s and 1930s, Josef Stalin attempted to purge his society of all religious belief. This was done through suppression: discriminatory laws were enacted, members of the clergy were executed, and the religious citizenry were terrified. While these measures drastically crippled religious institutions, they were ineffective at completely eliminating the idea of religion. Beliefs and traditions were passed down in communities clandestinely throughout the repressive rule of Stalin. After the fall of the Soviet Union, it became clear that religion had survived all along.

We see throughout literature and history that ignoring ideas and distracting people from them is generally more effective than to attempt to stamp an idea out through means of suppression. Authoritarian rule, in fact, can do the opposite: by dramatizing and calling attention to an idea in the name of condemning it, a regime might actually strengthen that idea.

Medium/Low Quality:

We have seen different governments try to crush out ideas throughout history. However, they are never actually successful in doing so. An idea can be ignored or suppressed, but it will never really go away. This is illustrated in the survival of religion in the Soviet Union.

In Soviet Russia during the 1920s and 1930s, Josef Stalin attempted to purge the society of all religious belief. This was done through suppression: discriminatory laws, execution of the clergy, and use of terror. While this harmed religious institutions, they were ineffective at crushing the idea of religion. Beliefs and traditions were passed down in communities secretly throughout the rule of Stalin. After the fall of the Soviet Union, it became clear that religion had survived all along.

The same kind of thing happened with apartheid law in South Africa. Even though there were laws against black Africans and white Africans using the same facilities, the idea caught fire, especially because of an international outcry against the law.

We see throughout history that suppressing ideas does not crush them. Authoritarian rule, in fact, can do the opposite: by calling attention to an idea in the name of condemning it, a regime might actually strengthen that idea.

Final Thoughts

In the end, we know that you will be successful in taking the FSOT. Although the road ahead may at times be challenging, if you continue your hard work and dedication (just like you are doing to prepare right now!), you will find that your efforts will pay off.

If you are struggling after reading this book and following our guidelines, we sincerely hope that you will take note of our advice and seek additional help. Start by asking friends about the resources that they are using. If you are still not reaching the score you want, consider getting the help of a FSOT tutor for whichever section you feel you are struggling with.

If you are on a budget and cannot afford a private tutoring service, there are plenty of independent tutors, including college students who are proficient in FSOT subjects. You don't have to spend thousands of dollars to afford a good tutor or review course.

We wish you the best of luck and happy studying. Most importantly, we hope you enjoy your coming years – after all, you put a lot of work into getting there in the first place.

Sincerely,
The Trivium Team

CPSIA information can be obtained at www.ICGtesting.com
Printed in the USA
LVOW05s0347300813

350319LV00008B/66/P